The Sand Castle

by Sela Greenblatt
illustrated by Bernard Adnet

HOUGHTON MIFFLIN HARCOURT
School Publishers

Printed in China

ISBN-13: 978-0-547-02732-6
ISBN-10: 0-547-02732-X

3 4 5 6 7 8 0940 18 17 16 15 14 13 12 11 10

Marcelo sat on the beach and looked at the big world around him.

"The sky is so wide," he said. "The clouds are so large. The waves are so tall!"

Marcelo looked down at himself. He felt very small.

Just then, the wind blew a big
ball across the beach. It hit
Marcelo and sent him flying
across the sand.

"That does it!" said Marcelo.
"I may look small, but I am
going to do something big. . .
something really big!"

Marcelo thought and thought.
Then an idea popped into
his ==head==.

"I'll build a sand castle! It
will be the biggest castle ever."

Marcelo got right to work.
He scooped some sand, added
water, then dumped it out.
The sand stood up by itself!

Marcelo worked hard. His castle was going to be HUGE!

Then Marcelo heard a loud roar. A big wave rose up and then—SPLASH! It flooded his castle. When the wave rolled away, all that was left was a mound of wet sand.

"Nooooooo!" shouted Marcelo.
His friends came over to see
what was wrong.

"I was making the biggest
sand castle in the world," said
Marcelo sadly. "Now I just have
a lump on the beach."

6

"You should build another castle!" said Bird. "Make it farther from the water. Then the waves won't reach it."

Marcelo shook his head. "I'm too small for such a big job."

"We're all small," said Crab. "But we can do a big job if we work together."

Everyone nodded. Marcelo grinned.

"Let's make the biggest sand castle ever!" said Marcelo.

They found a new spot and began building. One wall of the castle fell down.

"Don't worry," said Marcelo's mouse friend Marta. "We'll find a way to fix it."

"This sand is too dry," said
Marta. She added more water
and built the wall a second time.
It stood strong and tall.

Bird used her beak to peck out
windows and doors.

"Great work!" <mark>cried</mark> Marcelo.
He climbed the castle and shouted,
"I have the world's biggest sand
castle!"

Marcelo saw his friends smiling
up at him. He shouted even louder,
"I have the world's best friends!"

10

Responding

Story Structure

Who is this story about? Where does the story happen? What happens in the story? Make a chart.

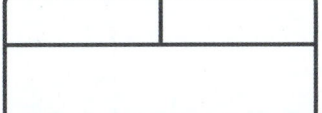

✏ Talk About It

Text to Text Think of another story about friends who had a problem. Do you think the friends in that story worked together? Tell what you think and why.

WORDS TO KNOW

across	head	second
ball	heard	should
cried	large	

LEARN MORE WORDS

flooded	mound	scooped

TARGET SKILL **Story Structure**

Tell the setting, character, and events in a story.

TARGET STRATEGY **Infer/Predict**

Use clues to figure out more about story parts.

GENRE A **fantasy** is a story that could not happen in real life.